AUTISM

AND AUTONOMY AT HOME

TOILET TRAINING

A parental guide to teaching autonomy at home and creating good routines for your child with autism

TABLE OF CONTENT

PREAMBLE

This book is intended to guide you throughout your child's toilet training; it will provide you with the basis for understanding how you can help your child achieve autonomy. Using the toilet is part of the set of skills necessary for social life; it has to be worked on and developed until it is acquired, so that eventually, your child won't need anybody to help him keep his dignity in his everyday life.

You will pave the way towards your child's success

Let's face it: nobody wishes to toilet train people's children after a certain age. Child minders, teachers, educators... all will tell you at a certain stage that they cannot go any further.

Why can't they? It is definitely not laziness on their part! This is just because some actions must remain within the private sphere, or performed by an appropriately trained person whose job and duty are to provide these particular sorts of services. However, you are currently reading this book because you are willing to help your child to be toilet trained before you get to such an extreme situation!

You will use your expertise on your child, his tastes, his desires, his knowledge, and his skills, so that you can adapt and tailor the strategies you will find in this book. Personalization is integral to achieving success.

Some strategies can also be used for purposes other than toilet training at home, but I will not deal with these situations in this book.

Some examples to help illustrate

You will find in this book my own personal views and experiences on this issue, with examples concerning my sons Matthieu and Julien, and a number of testimonials I have heard throughout the years.

You may already be familiar with most strategies I will mention. It is very difficult to say exactly what is going to work or not for your child: toilet training is a sort of trial and error process, in which you always try to keep everything that works well and abandon what does not... until next time.

Some children will be toilet trained quickly; others will keep on soiling themselves for months or maybe for years, if you are really unlucky.

Nonetheless you have no choice; it has to be done if you want your child to be toilet trained some day, for urine and stool, both during the day and the night.

Ask yourself the following question: would you prefer to have a tough time for a year or two, when your child is still young and you can still guide him physically or take him to the shower when he is soiled, or would you rather keep your child in diapers and clean him until the end of his life (or yours)?

My choice was made quickly, and even though I had a hard time with my sons, these efforts eventually paid off. So come and join the victorious side, those who won the war against the wet and soiled underwear!

You are super-parents

Many people are stingy with their encouragement and congratulations; I am not. I am convinced that your actions will pay off and improve the quality of your daily life significantly. Simply purchasing this book to help your child become independent proves that you are wonderful parents who are concerned with your child's well-being and future.

Many people around you will demoralize you: they will tell you this is pointless, that this is not your job, that if they were in your position they would have already given up, that you will have time to think about it later on. If you give up, you are sure to fail indeed! You cannot win the lottery if you don't try your luck!

Becoming independently, fully toilet trained is a crucial step for your child's future life. If not toilet trained, how will he go to school? How will he get a job? How will he just have fun with his friends, how will he raise a family? Our children are not all destined to live "normal" lives, but it does not mean that they should not approach this normality and live a life of happiness and dignity. This life that we all wish for them requires autonomy and toilet training.

Roll up your sleeves!

Bring along your household cleaners, clip an imaginary clothespin on your nose, and keep a few piles of underwear and extra clothes close at hand: let's start toilet training your child!

Best regards,
Nathalie Aynié

ADVISORY

Before we begin...

Toilet teaching is never achieved without some blood, sweat and tears, not to mention the fair number of atrocities that we, as parents of children with autism, have had experienced for the long weeks, months or years we spent trying to toilet train our child.

This book will help you toilet train your child, but its pages include many horror stories: you will read about urine, faeces, explosive diarrhea. In short, you will read about poop and pee.

Well, I would tell you "sensitive souls should stay away!" But I know you have been, or currently are buried up to your neck into faeces, with your hands and feet tied; otherwise you would not be reading these pages.

Put aside your disgust and embark on the toilet training adventure: you will have a hard time; you will find diapers are a thousand times more advantageous; you will give up every evening then buck up every morning. But it is definitely worthwhile!

So come on, we're going to make it together!

INTRODUCTION

Matthieu became fully toilet trained, both during the day and the night, at the age of 5, after many successive attempts and failures. Five years of hell.

Matthieu has hyposensitivity issues, therefore he did not mind remaining soiled for hours at night, or letting his diaper overflow and causing a "disastool" on his sheets and his clothes. Neither did he mind to touch his poop and spread it onto the wall or over him, nor to put it—yuck!—into his mouth. If I'd ever failed to be the world's most watchful mother, it would have been a complete disas-turd!

To be the mother of a child with autism also implies to take upon yourself, be strong and keep yourself from vomiting while you are cleaning out the a-poo-calypses , your imaginary clothespin firmly clipped on your nose!

I faced every imaginable refusal: refusal to remove his clothes, to sit on the toilet, to sit while he relieved himself... Every day my son's shrill cries of desperation would let the neighbours know exactly when I was taking him to the toilet.

Last summer, I repeated this experience with Julien, my four-year-old younger son. I cannot say I saw life through rose-coloured glasses (it was brown-coloured glasses instead) before he finally learned to use the toilet. The strategies used for Matthieu had worked for some time, which gave me the opportunity to revisit them before starting to write this book, but I had to be twice as ingenious and careful because of Julien's many refusals and outbursts of anger. This highlights how different every child is, even among siblings!

Armed with this new information and these two hard-fought victories, I suggest that you too embark on the toilet training adventure. Good luck!

GENERAL PRINCIPALS OF THE AYNIÉ METHOD

To begin with, if the title of my chapter had made you laugh, this is a good start. Keeping your sense of humour even in the midst of adversity will help you hold out and live better: you are on the right track!

I admit it seems a little conceited to give my own name to a method, but I've always had an offbeat sense of humour; besides I thought it might be a good way to differentiate between the purists of the ABA, TEACCH, PECS and other "acknowledged" methods, and those like me who would rather mix them all, then add a pinch here and there of whatever might be useful for their child and leave the rest.

Therefore, you DO have my full and complete permission to start with my method and use it to develop your own and give it your own name.

This method will exactly suit your child, and to develop it, you will have to focus on everything that works with him and allows him to improve.

To simplify things, I will keep the "Aynié method" name, particularly because I will speak about my own experience with Matthieu; but bear in mind that you will have to adapt it to be your method, not mine, in the future.

For example, Matthieu loves being congratulated, and I usually do not really need to present any food reinforcement to encourage him to work. If it's different with your child, use food treats!

Now, let me tell you something very important: your child is unique. His personality is unique, his tastes are unique, his skills and knowledge are unique, and comparing him with other children, autistic or not, will not ultimately be helpful.

He is himself, he is his own person, he deserves that we consider his particular case when we work or live with him.

Therefore, I suggest that you try the Aynié method if your child is not under the supervision of a professional for behavioral problems.

Adaptation on a case-by-case basis

As I just said, your child is unique. His differences requires a program based on "haute couture" standards, not just "ready-to-wear," or even "tailor-made" programs! He needs something outstanding that will help him succeed with flying colours!

The Aynié method is focused on finding a program that will fit your particular child like a glove by asking you to adapt the exercises to your child's strengths, weaknesses and tastes.

The never-ending task of building of a knowledge base

You can work effectively only on what you can understand well. True, you can achieve results by pure guesswork or gut instinct, but that involves a lot of risks and unnecessary detours.

Since there isn't just one type of autism but a spectrum, and any person with ASD is unique, different from others, not everything you will read in resource books will necessary apply to your child. But learning about the various types of autism will help you better understand your child, those unique parts of him that spring from his disability.

Even after several years, I am still learning and gathering information about all aspects of autism, even those not applicable to Matthieu; I read scientific publications, I listen to personal experiences, and I think about some issues in our lives or the lives of other people who are involved in our autism online community.

So the Aynié method encourages parents to read and learn as much as they can about autism.

A step-by-step teaching

I was speaking recently to a friend whose daughter has autism. She told me she did not know where to start. She was intimidated by the huge amount of work to be done and, seeing what we were doing with our children, she was wondering where to begin and how she could find time to work with her daughter work as much as we do with our sons.

It is just that we already have set up a basis to make our children work. Its implementation has been a slow process, and at first, it required a lot of effort for very few results. It's the same case for everyone! If autism were an easy ride, we would know it already.

Depending on each child's skills and abilities to adapt, the slightest exercise may be extremely easy to do or seem completely impossible.

One child may be fine sitting on the potty without any fuss; another won't. One child may be fully toilet trained quickly, whereas you'll have to keep a constant eye on another to prevent "accidents." One child will learn a skill quickly, whereas for another it will take weeks before he can start to develop what he has learned.

Therefore, you shouldn't hesitate to start with one or two major skills at a time, no more, and focus on them until acquisition, then only afterwards introduce other skills.

But even once the child has acquired a skill, it is important to review and require it regularly and perhaps even to go back over it and focus on it again if you find that he does not continue to show progress or he is reluctant to do it.

Only when the bases of obedience and autonomy are acquired, can you begin to teach more skills and introduce more of them each time, depending on your child's limit.

Tenacity with a hint of moderation

When to persevere? When to give up? Sometimes, learning seems to be so difficult for our children that we wonder whether we should give up: are they really able to do that? Is their disability preventing them from understanding or working?

When to give up? Never! You have to remain determined, you have to keep suggesting the activity to your child tirelessly, explaining the instructions over and over again, until he makes progress.

However, you have to be measured in your actions. It is better not to start anything if you don't feel courageous enough to continue to face your child's refusal, for hours if necessary, or if you feel that your child is not ready yet.

Just because your friend's child successfully performs an activity does not mean your child is ready to do so. He may lack the development skills necessary to achieve the exercise.

When you start an exercise, you have to suggest it to your child regularly, several times a day, until it is perfectly learned.

Once you've asked your child to do an exercise, you must not give up if he does not want to finish it. Give it serious thought: are you ready to spend hours on it if your child refuses to do it? Are you ready to hear him screaming, to be forcefully pushed away?

We are not far from psychological war, but none of your requests must be ignored, so that your child will get used to working whenever you ask him to.

It is up to you to decide when it is worth starting an exercise or making a request and when it would be better to do nothing.

How to choose good routines

Basically, routines are bad for autistic children. They often cannot tolerate change, and once a routine is established, it is very difficult to uninstall it: the child will have crying fits or temper tantrums, or he will just go back to his old routine despite your strict rule against it.

Everything has to be done to disrupt all the bad routines: the time-consuming ones, those that cause the child to stereotype, and those that may prove dangerous.

For example, if your child absolutely needs to flush the toilet, at least once, as soon as he gets into the bathroom, this routine must be disrupted mercilessly, otherwise it's very likely to become an "I flush twice before and twice after" routine, and then you will have to start from scratch if you want to prevent him from doing it.

Conversely, do not hesitate to introduce what we will call "good routines": washing hands after using the toilet, making sure his bottom is clean before getting dressed, turning the light on and off properly, etc.

Generalization

Once the exercise is completed, it is not enough to just give it a good rating and move on. The child must be able to do the same thing again:

- Regularly,

- Outside the house,

- At different times,

- With a different person,

- Under different circumstances.

But it is easier to move forwards; if you know that the child has already achieved the exercise, then you must rely on his previous achievement to encourage him to generalize the skills he has acquired.

When NOT to use the Aynié method

If you are fortunate enough to be supervised by professionals such as a behavioural psychologist, if you are taught TEACCH or PECS and the people involved in your child's education are board certified (one does not become a behavioural psychologist overnight, nor claim to know PECS after having read three online articles on it), rely on what these professionals are telling you.

Behavioural programs for autistic people are expensive because the skills are long and difficult to learn and understand. Furthermore, real behavioural professionals are scarce. Whenever you are given advice, be all ears!

If you can successfully fulfil the necessary conditions for the program you have chosen (number of hours, compliance, number of professionals involved in the re-education program, financial resources, etc.), and if you want to use a method and give it a chance to make your child improve, then go all out!

But rely also on your instincts and on your own observations of the results.

If you notice that your child does not improve at all, in any area, after a consistent period of time, then ask yourself questions and try alternative methods. He may not be receptive to your current method, but that does not mean he will not respond to another one.

GETTING READY FOR TOILET TRAINING

Toilet training is a daunting task for parents as well as for children. For long weeks, and maybe for long months for the most unfortunate, you will have your hands in poop, a mop always leaning against the wall, and your laundry basket always overflowing with dirty laundry.

Do your best and prepare for potty training as much as possible; this will spare you many useless battles and disappointments.

Make sure you are familiar with the following issues:

Is my child ready to be toilet trained?

There are several factors that will let you know if your child has the physical and psychological skills to be toilet trained. It is generally said that it is best to wait until the child is at least 18 months old, or 18 months old in mental development, to successfully achieve toilet training.

Can he go up and down the stairs alone?

Going up and down the stairs unassisted may seem unrelated to toilet training, but if a child is able to walk up or down the stairs, that means he can control the muscles that will help him expel or hold himself when he goes to the toilet.

Does he look uncomfortable and let you know when he is soiled?

It is hard to make a child understand he must be clean if he can stay for hours in a dirty diaper and be quiet about it.

To encourage your child to feel uncomfortable when he is soiled, you have to be watchful and change his diaper regularly, soon after it is wet or soiled.

Your child will gradually get used to having his bottom dry, and he will feel uncomfortable whenever his diaper is dirty.

Does he have a varied diet?

A child with a somewhat unusual diet may suffer frequent diarrhea or, worse still, constipation, which will hamper the toilet training process. You might have to experiment with different foods and plan specific diets to help your child regulate stool hardness. It will be much simpler if your child eats everything.

Do you change his diaper at least six times a day?

Some children hold back, then relieve themselves and defecate at the same time, several times a day; others will urinate a small amount at a time, regularly, throughout the day. The latter are wet all the time and they cannot stay dry for more than one hour, which means they pee any time they feel the urge to. It demonstrates that they are not quite as ready as they should be to be toilet trained.

Is his diaper dry sometimes in morning?

This concerns mainly nighttime toilet training, but also demonstrates that he can control bladder function for a rather long time, which is a very good sign.

"Be prepared!"

Accidents often take us by surprise. That's how it is—otherwise they would not be accidents, since we could foresee them and anticipate them!

So you have to be just like the Scouts: always be prepared to act and react, in any situation! Here are a few useful things you should anticipate:

A change of clothes

You will need many spare clothes, especially in the beginning. The options are limited: either you buy enough clothes and underpants, or you use the washing-machine and the dryer regularly, according to your needs.

The summer is the best season for toilet training, because you dress your child less warmly. But if you live in a well-heated house or flat, you can start it whenever you want: you just need to leave your child bare-bottomed or in his underwear all day. Be sure, however, that this remains within the immediate family sphere, and that he does not interpret it as a permission to undress in public.

Cleaning products

At the beginning, most of the time, accidents occur frequently, because even if you are watchful it is difficult to anticipate when your child will pee.

Make sure that you've got cleaning products in such different strategic places as the bathroom. Also have a bucket and a mop, bleach cleaner, and a sponge dedicated to that particular use only, and always make sure they are available anywhere you and your child will go in your apartment or your house.

Why available anywhere? Because many of our children do not feel disgusted by their excretions, and if you go away to get what you need to clean up the mess, on your return, you are likely to find them with their hands in their poop or their pee. An ounce of prevention is worth a pound of cure!

Moreover, you can ask them to help you cleaning up. I will discuss this more in another chapter.

Hygiene products

Always keep a small basket full of cotton squares and hygiene products for children's bottoms in your bathroom and/or your toilet.

You must focus first and foremost on teaching him to use toilet paper to wipe himself (autonomously or with a little guidance from you), but you might have to resume cleaning with a suitable product, because excrement can be difficult to remove. Your child must feel the difference between being clean and being soiled if you want him to enjoy being clean.

Make your life easier (especially at nighttime)

As parents of children with autism, we all know how it feels to suffer from lack of sleep, exhaustion, to be irritated by too-short nights. You can be sure your little rascal will choose the exact moment when, at last, you close your eyes, to have a bowel movement and spread his poop all over his bed.

Taking your child to the shower, sometimes against his will, in the middle of the night: whoever dreamed we'd be doing this?

It is important for you to try to make your life the easiest possible in every way and especially at nighttime, so that you can sort it out even with your eyes half open and eventually go back into the arms of Morpheus.

Changing bed sheets

I have a nice trick that will change your lives when you have to change bed sheets at night: layers! Let me explain: you just need to use several layers of linen, a bed sheet over a waterproof draw sheet, then a bed sheet, then another draw sheet, a bed sheet, etc. Put two or three layers of them on the mattress, or even under it, so that you will just have turn it over if there is an accident.

Then you will just have to take off the wet or soiled bed linen and put your child back to bed; you won't have to go and get clean sheets and make the bed again in the middle of the night.

Provide changes of underwear in most places

It is primarily underwear and pajama bottoms that get wet or soiled at night, so keep some clean ones nearby in the child's bedroom or in the bathroom so that you can change his clothes quickly before you put him back to bed.

Provide some t-shirts and pajama tops too, because they might eventually get soiled; it would be unfortunate that you'd have to go to the other end of the house to get some clean ones from the pile of clothes waiting to be ironed.

Plan everything you need for your comfort

Toilet training might involve significant personal cost for autistic children and for their parents too, since they have to deal with the whole organisation and crisis management. It is important for you to find solutions which simplify your life and use them as often as possible.

For instance, put a bench or a chair in the toilet or the bathroom, so that you can sit down when your child is trying to put his trousers back on. Use lamps that provide low-intensity light to keep your child sleepy; if you have to help him go to sleep after you changed his clothes, your nights will never end.

Get everyone involved

If you are not the only parent looking after your child, it might be a good idea to organize night watching on a rotating basis. For example, mummy can go to bed early and daddy will deal with the toilet visits until midnight while fiddling with the computer; then mummy will wake up at one o'clock and take over it until seven. Or vice versa, according to what is more convenient to the family, on an equitable basis.

At school, you must ensure that your child's toilet training is monitored, that diapers are avoided as much as possible, and that trips to the bathroom are suggested to your child regularly instead of waiting him to express his needs.

Summon up your courage

Toilet training can be a very long process; it involves significant personal cost to parents, particularly to the mother who is often left alone to deal with trips to the bathroom, post-a-poo-calyptic showers, and soiled clothes and laundry washing.

Even though sometimes you will just want to run away from it all, you must go on. You might have a hard time for two years, but it means that in the end it will be over, you will never have to clean off poop from the walls and the floor any more.

It can only work if you keep it up. Every time you give up, you'll have to start all over again!

So stay "zen" as much as possible, and summon up courage. You can do it!

Avoid scolding all the time

There are too main reasons why you should avoid scolding your child if he has an accident and soils his clothes or his sheets.

First, he probably did not do it deliberately, so there is no point in shaming and scolding since this is something he still has no control over. Consider that these skills cannot be learned in a few days only, and that it takes real team work to help your child be toilet trained in the gentlest way possible.

Secondly, in the case of defiant behaviour, if your child soils himself deliberately to bother you, scolding him means giving him what he wants: your attention (even negative), and the satisfaction of seeing you react exactly as expected. In such cases, stay neutral; show no expression on your face. Take him to the toilet for as long as you need to quiet down.

Don't show him your disgust

I understand it is difficult. There is an a-poo-calypse in his underwear; it is hard to withhold a grimace. Yet, be careful! It is frustrating for a child to see that you are disgusted by his excretions.

There is some poop on the toilet seat? So what? At least, it is close to where he should relieve himself! Notice his progress, discuss the things he must improve next time, clean off the whole place and wait until your child is out of sight to express your disgust by making as many faces as you want.

Know how to react

If you don't scold him all the time, training will be much more efficient, especially if your anger does not weaken your wisdom. For example, make him understand that you are not happy because he has soiled himself, even though five minutes ago you suggested he to go to the toilet. If scolding is not something you do very often, the impact on the child will be greater.

You don't need to make a big fuss about it, either! Just speak to him simply, in an upset tone, and tell him, for example, that he must not leave the toilet until you are sure he has finished relieving himself.

THE STEPS TO TOILET TRAINING

Now I am going to introduce the different steps in your child's toilet training. Sometimes, they may be more or less difficult to reach, and your child may achieve them in a different order. Once they are all learned, then your child will be considered fully toilet trained.

Sitting on the toilet

Children with autism may refuse to sit on the toilet or on the training potty. It might be because it is a change, which they strongly resist, or because they are afraid, or because they just don't want to do it, or because they prefer to spend their time doing something else in some other place. For all these reasons, you might have to fight a long battle before your child eventually consents to sit on the toilet.

Physical guidance might be necessary at the beginning, so don't hesitate to ask a stronger person to help you hold the child when he's sitting on the toilet, at least for the first few times, so that he won't be able to wiggle around easily and slide down to the floor.

When your child decides to sit on the toilet without screaming or fighting, give him a reinforcer (use a food item if it was really difficult, a social item otherwise). When your child has got into the habit of sitting on the toilet, use fewer reinforcers, until you don't use any of them anymore.

Peeing on request

Throughout the day, you will regularly suggest trips to the bathroom to your child. If you don't suggest them every five minutes and choose reasonable time intervals, then he should urinate every time, even though it might be only a few drops.

Peeing on request means that the child has gained enough control of himself to eliminate urine even if he could have held back a bit longer. It can be useful before a long road trip, when you ask your child to go to the toilet before he gets into the car.

Asking to go to the toilet or going by himself?

Whether your child is verbal or non-verbal, he can learn how to ask for trips to the bathroom.

For verbal children, it could be an opportunity to work on requests, to introduce new vocabulary ("Well, you've drunk too much hot chocolate! Come on, let's go to the bathroom so that you can relieve yourself!"). Non-verbal children can be taught how to request by using a pictogram: the child brings in the toilet pictogram, and then the action is verbalized when you take him to the toilet (and ask him to repeat).

If the child can remove his clothes by himself, he can also learn to go to the toilet directly; then perhaps he can call you afterward to help him wipe himself properly and pull up his pants.

Learn to hold his urges

There is still a ten-minute drive to get home! Daddy is doing his crossword puzzles in the bathroom! Your child must learn to hold his urges, for short periods at first, then for longer periods. To work on it with him, you can ask him to keep on holding it in for another minute or another thirty seconds before you take him to the toilet.

Sometimes, the child requests to go to the toilet at the very last second and wets himself on his way. Learning to hold back can be useful in this case too.

To pee AND poop in the toilet

Many parents who achieved successfully their autistic children's toilet training will tell you: it is much harder to make them have a bowel movement than it is to make them urinate.

Pooping in the toilet is likely to occur long after you've successfully taught him to pee in the right place. You must be aware of that.

Nighttime cleanness

Achieving daytime cleanness does not mean that your nights will be quiet and restful. It requires a higher degree of maturity. It is generally advised that you take diapers off during the night as well as the day, but it seems to be very difficult, especially when the child is not ready and the parents are already exhausted. But if you have the courage, it is the best thing to do!

Otherwise, before you start nighttime training, you had better wait until your child is able to pee and a poop in the toilet and his diapers are always clean in the morning.

But even so, accidents may happen. Slight regressions are likely to occur before nighttime cleanness is fully acquired, so you'd better be prepared psychologically.

Generalization of toilet training

Your child is toilet trained at home? Great! But it is not over... He has to achieve cleanness at school too, and at other places you know, such as the speech therapist's office, the riding therapy centre, at grandpa and grandma's, etc.

Additionally, he has to be dry and clean even when you are not there. When the special needs assistant takes him to the toilet, your child must agree to go with him or her and relieve himself instead of holding it in all day long, which might cause accidents.

Therefore, it is very important to have other people involved in your child's toilet training. You must tell them that children with autism find it hard to generalize, so their help and assistance in your child's improvement are absolutely necessary.

Ideally, generalization has to be worked in parallel with any skills in which your child is improving:

- To sit on any toilet, whether you are there or not, or even on a potty if the toilet is inaccessible;
- To pee on request or to ask to do it, by making a verbal request or by using a picture;
- To hold back, in any place and at any time;
- And to relieve himself completely, even though

it is difficult because he cannot have as much privacy as at home.

With regard to passing stools, usually children as well as adults would rather wait to be back home to relieve themselves. This is no big deal, provided that in case of urgent need they are able to go to the toilet by themselves before they get soiled.

Additionally, some children are very sensitive to cleanliness of the toilet, so they can hold back in some places that have been poorly cleaned.

SOME ISSUES THAT YOU MIGHT HAVE TO DEAL WITH

If toilet training were as simple as gently sitting your child on the toilet, it would be wonderful! Unfortunately, it won't be that simple. The following pages outline the range of issues you might have to deal with and a few ideas to help you sort them out or figure out your own solutions.

Refusals

Your child won't: sit down, pee or poop, remove his/her clothes, go to the toilet, stop yelling, etc.

Refusals are almost inevitable, you have to weaken them before it gets too bad. For my part, all means are good, provided that the child eventually complies: promises, severity, cuddling, doggedness, earplugs, anything so that he finally does as requested. Once he gets into the habit of complying, things will be easier for you and you won't have to give him your precious iPhone to have fun with while he is on the toilet.

I think the reward should fit the difficulty the child had in complying. If your child is throwing a tantrum because he does not want to sit on the toilet, give him something that will make him stay on it. If he complies without much fuss, just congratulate him; it should be enough.

Overflowing

Your child, so eager to go back to the living room and play with his mountain of Legos ®, might have his little bottom wrongly positioned on the toilet seat. I experienced this type of "flooding" more than once, and I think it occurs regularly, particularly with little boys.

Don't hesitate to use a toilet seat insert so that your child can sit properly if your toilet seat is too big for him. Since he will have to go regularly, and sometimes to stay for a long time, we want him to be comfortable; if he feels uncomfortable, he just won't stay seated.

Routines

Children with autism are slaves to their routines. Sometimes you'll have to uninstall them to prevent them from becoming too overwhelming.

Going to the toilet as soon as he arrives somewhere

As a precaution, I used to ask Matthieu to go to the toilet every time we arrived somewhere. So, thereafter, even though he was perfectly able to hold back for several hours when at home, he would go to the toilet every half an hour when we were away from home. This was caused by his habit of going to the toilet every time we arrived at his therapy sessions.

Therefore, sometimes I refused to let him go to the toilet at these moments. Why not all the time? Because I don't want to let a new routine settle (not going to the toilet anymore, going every two days, going only on Fridays, etc.)

Having overwhelming rituals

You have to be particularly watchful of these rituals. This way of controlling everything may seem tough and strict. But it is necessary if you want to help your child; otherwise he may throw a tantrum every time you don't let him flush the toilet twice after every visit, he may scream because you wouldn't let him throw three sheets of toilet paper exactly in the toilet bowl, and many other joys tailored-made by your child himself, which will just drive you crazy.

Furthermore, these rituals tend to multiply. So if you don't want to find yourself with your child requesting thirty-six toilet flushings and twenty-three switch-flippings every time he goes to the toilet, you will have to watch all this closely.

Confusions

Our children are smart, yet sometimes things that seem extremely simple to us might be a bit confusing in their minds. Here is a list of confusions that might occur, and of which you have to be watchful.

Confusion between diapers and underpants

My children used to mistake diapers with underwear. They felt their bottoms were wrapped and protected, so they relieved themselves in their underpants, and then were surprised they got wet.

During the summer, I took the opportunity to leave them bare-bottomed and toilet trained them during the time we were at home. Obviously this was not embarrassing for young children, but try to do the same thing with a pre-adolescent and you will most likely have, or cause, trouble.

They must be reminded constantly that they are not in diapers and they must relieve themselves in the toilet, whether they have diapers on for safety or not.

Confusion between cotton and toilet paper

I often keep a packet of cotton squares in the bathroom, with cleaning products for babies' bottoms, because sometimes toilet paper is not enough to wipe off excrement. However, over time, I've needed them less and less, so I've put them out of the bathroom to avoid problems.

Because problems might occur indeed, particularly when the younger ones want to do the right thing and use ten cotton squares and a third of the bottle of cleaning product to wipe themselves instead of calling for help.

Our toilet have become clogged and flooded several times because of that. So be careful! If you can, the best thing to do is to put the cotton and product in a place where you can access them, but they are out of reach of younger children. If you want them to be autonomous anyway, watch your children and control their use.

Escape behaviours

Our children always have something to do before complying: finishing reading their story, drinking a glass of water, tidying up their soft toys, throwing their Legos® on the ground to be scolded instead of doing this boring activity that keeps them stuck in the toilet for several minutes.

In addition to these distractions, there might be physical escape that forces us to run after a little bare-bottom goblin who runs away from us immediately after being undressed.

These are behaviours you will have to know and foresee, and with experience, it will be easier and easier for you to stop them. Cheer up! Don't let your child take advantage of you: he will have to learn to be clean; there is no other alternative.

Spreading of excrements

Our autistic children often are hypersensitive or hyposensitive. Hyposensitivity causes them not to feel disgusted by their excrements, so that you might eventually find your child happily covered with poop, and spreading more of it on the wall or all over his bed—something that would make you go bananas.

You must be aware that this might happen: what used to be relatively confined by the diaper might become an experimental device in our little angels' hands.

You must, by all means, explain to him that this is disgusting and he cannot do that. Describe the principles of hygiene to them, teach them to call you if they poop instead of playing with it. Your relentless fight will be the only way to achieve some results in such situations.

TECHNIQUES

Here is a series of techniques applicable to your autistic child's toilet training. Now, it is up to you to optimise their efficiency by combining and adapting them to your child's personality.

Always have a time timer on hand

This is useful for both of you. A timer will provide you with an alarm every time you'll have to take your child to the toilet.

When I was toilet training my children, I used my computer's alarm. At the beginning, it rang every half hour, because of the frequent accidents, then every hour, then every hour and half. I stopped using it when I realised that my children went to the toilet by themselves, or asked to be taken.

If I forgot to set the time timer, the same thing would inevitably occur: I was overwhelmed by my current task, washing the dishes or writing my articles, or even posting on Facebook, and I would forget about the time. And an accident inevitably occurred! Since then, I learned not to forget time anymore.

The timer is useful to children too, because the time spent in the toilet might seem long to them, and the timer provides them an indication of how long they have to wait before they can go back to their preferred activity.

Using reinforcers

Many reinforcers may help you in your quest for toilet training. Usually, the most efficient ones are food items, which disturb many moms who are scared that cakes and sweets become the only way to make their children compliant; they are also afraid that their children will become obese. But the benefit of reinforcers is that they help children understand that they can achieve a given activity. Later on, they are fazed out over time, gradually but fairly quickly, and some of them are replaced by other reinforcers (i. e. social reinforcers such as congratulations).

Here is a list of reinforcers you'll have to know and use to help your child be toilet trained:

Continuous reinforcers

Use them when he successfully learns to sit on the toilet seat. It can be a story, a song, a book, a video, a game available in the toilet only, etc.

In short, you can use anything, that helps make toilet time as pleasant as possible. It has to be something your child enjoys so much that he will comply to get this reinforcer.

Final reinforcers

To be used sparingly! Before starting toilet training, make a list of all the items your child particularly enjoys, items for which he would do anything. For example, Matthieu enjoyed sticking coloured stickers, but he would have done anything for a sweet.

Bear in mind that these reinforcers may change according to the age. Sweets are no longer final reinforcers for Matthieu, by the way; he has become so compliant that I would not be able to tell you which reinforcer would currently work for him, since I don't need to use them anymore (such social reinforcers as congratulations work pretty well with him).

This type of reinforcer has to be used only in cases of first achievements: first pee, first poop. It must be provided in these very specific situations, otherwise your child will conclude he can perform anything else and get the reinforcer from you, and he won't be motivated for toilet training. Keep these final reinforcers for the current task, so that you child will be motivated to work on it.

Social reinforcers

Social reinforcers are congratulations, of course! Tell him that you are proud of him, applause, make up a little song to praise his achievement, call granddad and granny to tell them how kind, how beautiful, how smart, how compliant he is...

Social reinforcers must gradually replace the other types of reinforcers. Your child's actions must become gradually "normal" actions that may not require necessarily a whole celebration and whole paraphernalia of reinforcers.

Over time, you will have to reinforce on some occasions only, or when he brilliantly achieved a particularly difficult activity.

Learn to choose your reinforcers

The reinforcing objects must fit in the bathroom, should not be easily damaged, they must be easy to clean, and they must not be too big, or too small so that they won't end up in the toilet (or clogging it up).

Watch for reinforcers that might be too powerful: if your child loves to play with handheld game console and you give it to him when he goes to the toilet only, then he might spend hours in the toilet. This is not the intended purpose, particularly when someone else needs to go.

Use behaviour charts

It's always good to measure your child's progress. You can, at the same time, make it an educational and entertaining activity for your child!

For example: a chart with the days of the week. Your child sticks a yellow sticker each time he pees, and a blue one each time he poops. If he has an accident, you stick a red one (don't let him do it, otherwise you will reinforce the accident). This device will enable him to learn the days of the week, to stick and unstick stickers (these activities develop fine motor skills, which are very difficult to achieve for children with autism), to focus on instruction only (learning to wait and follow the instruction, and not trying to stick thirty-six stickers at a time).

From one day to the next, and most importantly, from one week to the next, you will be able to compare and notice the improvements in your child's toilet training.

Exploiting routines

We have already touched on this subject: a child with autism is often ruled by his routines. Usually, they must be uninstalled before they become too overwhelming.

Conversely, you can also use the autistic children's need for routines to his own benefit.

Compulsory toilet visits

You can introduce infrequent but useful compulsory bathroom visits, to make sure your child will use the toilet regularly during the day.

At home there are compulsory bathroom visits: upon waking in the morning, after lunch, after the nap (or "quiet time") and in the evening, before going to bed. Between these times, the child can choose any time he finds appropriate to relieve himself, as often as necessary. We also try to encourage toilet visits just before we go out for a long time to avoid accidents in the car.

Guidance

Physical, verbal or visual guidance must be provided when needed only, and these must be fazed out as quickly as possible. If you keep on providing him with guidance all the time, your child will never be able to achieve anything by himself, and he will always need to be told what he must do.

Physical guidance

Your child cannot do or does not want to do the requested action? Help him in his movements by gently but firmly taking him and make him perform it.

For example: your child does not want to sit on the toilet? Place him on the toilet seat and hold him until he quiets down. Your child cannot drop his trousers? Place yourself behind him, grab his hands, make him put his thumbs against the waistband and help him drop it down.

Always add verbal guidance to this physical guidance.

Verbal guidance

Try to keep verbal guidance to a minimum. At the beginning, break down any action into sequences for your child, but let him gradually find the following logical action by himself.

Always keep in mind the necessity of using simple words, especially if your child has serious communication impairments. Additionally, always try to use simple words or sentences whenever you can, to make his understanding easier.

Verbal guidance must replace physical guidance quickly, then it has to be fazed out too, otherwise you might have to repeat the sequences to your child over and over again for all his life (and yours).

Visual guidance

When they have to do difficult things, it is often hard for autistic children to remember logical continuations (first we do x, then we do y, then only after that we do z). This is why sometimes we find them sitting on the toilet seat with their trousers on, on the verge of disaster, or with trousers back on but bottom unclean.

You can set up a series of visual sequences to help him understand in which order the actions are linked together, using pictures, or words if he can read already. Then you will gradually remove visual guidance for actions he has understood, so that he can be fully independent.

Require compliance

When an order is given, you must not give in. This is why you must be ready to struggle until the child complies and obeys your order. Otherwise, he will understand that when he shouts and screams, when he hits and rolls around on the ground, then you will give up, and he will win. He will take advantage of it; he will do the same thing every time and will not want to do what you ask him to.

Don't give in if he screams and hits

If your child does not comply within the few seconds following your request, direct him physically.

If you are not very strong, ask your husband, your brother, your cousin, your neighbour or your friend's husband to help you for the first times. He should intervene only in cases of big difficulties: you don't want your child to listen to you only when he is here.

When they don't want to do something, autistic children are capable of spectacular behaviour bursts. Don't let them influence you: stay strong!

Improving the chances of successful toilet training

To improve the chances of getting good results, you can increase the daily toilet visits too. Here's how.

Increase their water intake

When your child pees in the toilet successfully, reward him with a quarter glass of water, milk, syrup, juice or soda. This should not go on for too long, and to avoid giving him too much sugar, focus on low-sugar drinks. But it must be party time anyway!

Reinforcer and guidance fading

Fade reinforcers as quickly as possible, that is as soon as:

- Actions are less demanding for your child (he complies without complaining too much);

- Your child does what you ask him to do regularly: for example, after five final reinforcers, reward only one time in two when he pees, and thereafter tell him that this reinforcer will be given to him when he poops in the toilet.

This fading is intended to ensure that when he is 40 years old, your child won't still ask for strawberry ice-cream each time he visits the toilet -- and consequently, won't be overweight. Similarly, social reinforcers must gradually disappear: can you imagine yourself dancing and singing in the toilet at the age of 80 to congratulate your adult son or daughter because he has been toilet trained?

Some autistic children with a serious disability may need visual guidance all their lives.

TECHNICAL SUPPORTS

There are so many things to say about toilet training! You will find in the following pages a few things you should know before you start, to make your task easier and increase your chances of success.

Be inflexible

An autistic child is inflexible; therefore, you have to be inflexible too. I would even go further: you have to be even more stubborn and tenacious than he is.

Never giving up, not even for a single day

Once you have decided that your child will not wear diapers anymore, don't put him back in diapers! There will be times with no trouble at all; they will alternate with a-poo-calyptic times when you will want to give up everything. Don't! Hold on!

Try to choose a period of time that you will devote to this exclusively: holidays, summertime, or a few months when you will be less demanding about other skills. A child cannot always learn everything at the same time, even though some of them are doing pretty well!

Ensuring that "accidents" are onerous to the child

Ah, obviously, it is much more fun for him to keep on playing with his Legos® than spend time in the toilet. But if you force the child to clean up after the accident, it will turn out to be much more onerous. Therefore, once he has understood, it will be much simpler for him to go to the toilet rather than having to clean up everything.

Handling anguish

Sitting on the toilet may cause anguish to an autistic child. I haven't been able to calm my sons with these methods, but I've been told they have worked pretty well with other children, so I provide them to you.

Describe how the human body functions

Why do we pee and poop? Where do they come from? What are they for? There are a number of very good books on how the human body functions that provide answers. They can be used as stories that work as a continuous reinforcer while your child is sitting on the toilet.

Explain where the faeces and urine go

Autistic children may be anguished when they see "a part of themselves" go into the toilet. It is not me who says this: it is psychoanalysis, but I guess it is true for some of them, isn't it?

Anyway, it cannot do any harm to explain to them that it is not a part of themselves; after you have explain how the human body functions, tell them it is just the food parts that his body does not need, so there is nothing wrong with it, and the same thing happens to everybody.

Don't be afraid to make a lot of fuss about it: tell them how his poop will join its parents, its brothers and sisters, its cousins and the rest of the family!

Show him what happens when you go to the toilet

I'm not a huge fan of this method either, because I'd rather enjoy privacy when I go to the bathroom. But if the example of your bathroom visit can help your child understand what you ask him to do, I would say "Why not?"

But don't forget to tell your child how important it is for him to keep his privacy, so he has to close the door when he goes to the toilet.

Explain why it is important for him to be clean

Your child probably sees only disadvantages to toilet training: it takes up a lot of his time, and he has to make effort to do something he does not want to do and he does not necessarily understand.

Give him enjoyable reasons to be clean, if there is something good for him at stake, it will generate a lot of motivation:

- If you are clean, you will be allowed to go to the swimming pool with your brother and your sister;

- If you are clean, you will be allowed to go to school more often;

- If you are clean, it means you are a big boy/girl, therefore you will be allowed to (a privilege he is really excited about which you have never granted him so far).

Dedicate a special time for the poop

Matthieu used to associate toilet visits with peeing, so he would not sit on the toilet seat for more than two or three minutes, and if I forced him a stay longer, he did not understand why.

So we decided to introduce a special toilet time for poop: he was allowed to pee too if he wanted to, but he had to poop, and could not leave until he did it. The three or four first times went on for a long while, but he eventually understood that he had to have a bowel movement at that moment. Then he generalized, so now he can poop anytime during his toilet visits.

Make him recognize signs of discomfort

Your child is wriggling on the floor? Take a couple of minutes to make him aware that it is because he has an urge to pee. Then he will be able to associate these signs of discomfort with the necessity of going to the toilet.

TRICKS

There are thousands of tricks that you can use to encourage your child to behave properly and comply with trips to the bathroom and to help make them easier. Over time, you will find out your own tricks, and the most appropriate ones.

In the meanwhile, you will find here a number of useful tricks to help you start toilet training.

Choose clothes that make the process easier

Yes indeed, your little rascal or your little princess is sooooo cute when dressed up in their little clothes full of buttons, with belts and suspenders, and so many frills that you can hardly count them!

We are obviously all very proud, but they may not be the most appropriate clothes for toilet training.

I would recommend sweatpants or skirts with an elastic waistband to simplify your child's task. It is difficult to teach them to drop their pants quickly enough so as not to soil themselves; let's not make it even more difficult!

Once toilet training is finished, when they are able to hold themselves, you will have plenty of time to teach him how to button up his clothes, put on his belt, lace up her shoes up. Then you will be able to dress them the way you want. In the meanwhile, let's make it fast and easy!

Warn the child a bit before

Autistic children have great difficulty with changes. For a long time, Matthieu had fits of anger every time I wanted him to change activities.

I noticed that warning him a bit before asking him to go to the toilet helped him accept transition: so I set the timer five minutes before, and I warned him that he had to go to the toilet five minutes later. It usually works pretty well when he is warned before.

Bring a piece of his activity

Your child finds it difficult to leave his game anyway? Allow him from time to time to take either the whole game or a piece of it, with him to the toilet. It will help make the transition easier until toilet training is completed. However, it must not become a habit! It is up to you to find the right balance.

Check the toilet before flushing

Find a ploy to prevent your child from flushing the toilet before you have checked them.

Putting an object on the flush handle did not hide it from my son, so I found another solution: I closed the toilet tank tap so that it has no water in it the next time, and I opened it again, temporarily, just enough to fill the tank before I flushed again.

Prefer toilet to potty

You can find very efficient and comfortable toilet seat inserts for young children. There are many reasons why I preferred to use the toilet rather than the potty:

- Practicality: no need to empty the potty twenty times a day;

- Hygiene: when you have experienced the potty knocked over and excrement spilled and scattered everywhere in the living room by a pair of dirty little feet, you enjoy the comfort provided by toilet;

- The risk that he gets into the habit: if your autistic child gets fixated, refuses to use the toilet and requests the potty, you will be very much annoyed since you will have to re-teach everything from the beginning.

Toilet seat inserts are rather cheap and they easily adapt to all toilets. Furthermore, your child will be higher, so he will be within your reach easily for bottom-wiping and physical guidance sessions.

Tell your child he is a big boy/girl now

Being toilet trained means making a step further towards autonomy, growing up. There must be rewards for him at this stage, so that the child realizes that it is cool to be big, because he is granted more privileges; but there are a number of actions he has to do, and he must learn to do them by himself, or with a little help from dad and mom at the beginning.

No changing table anymore

Changing tables are for babies. Oh, I understand, it was infinitely more practical for you, but this time is over: your child has to learn to wipe his bottom by himself, to get dressed by himself, and he must do it standing up just like the grown-ups.

Prevent some routines

Many routines and silly things can be done, even in such bare spaces as toilet. Rely on my long experience!

Put the toilet lid down when flushing

It prevents the child from stereotyping before the toilet whirlpool. Try to restrict the number of toilet flushings too, because they might become a game.

Keep the toilet paper roll away from him

There are several situations:

- The child finds the toilet paper roll and thinks it might be fun to push it into the toilet;

- The child tries to wipe himself, drops the roll, which unwinds on the floor as he is pulling the toilet paper. He eventually cuts off the paper, stuffs 65 feet of paper with a drop of pee into the toilet and clogs the toilet drain.

You have to be watchful, and the first times leave only a few sheets of toilet paper available to your child (let's say three or four sheets).

Tell him he does not need to use them all at once, one or two sheets are enough, unless he has pooped.

Remove all sources of distraction

Remove from the bathroom any object which might distract your child's attention from his purpose. Autistic children are smart, and they will use any excuse to focus on something else than the current task, which in this case is learning to relieve themselves in the toilet.

OTHER SKILLS TO ACQUIRE

With toilet training, you will have to teach your autistic child other skills which are not necessarily easy for him.

To undress himself

It's much easier than putting his clothes back on, particularly if you have chosen practical clothes for him. You will have to show him how to drop his pants (or her skirt) and his underwear.

To wipe his bottom by himself

You will have to direct your child physically at the beginning to teach him the movements. Make him hold the toilet paper sheets, then direct his hand so that you do the right movement with him, then let him do it by himself and correct his gesture if he can't. After a while, he will have to do it alone, and even if it is not quite clean, you will have to accept it and intervene only if it is too soiled.

Do I give him cleansing wipes instead of toilet paper?

This is a double-edged sword. On one hand, it is more convenient for your child to wipe himself. On the other hand, wipes must be thrown in the garbage, not in the toilet, which makes another situation that your child has to understand and learn to do.

I think that you are the only one who can determine whether it is a good or a bad idea. For my part, I keep cotton squares and cleaning products for skin and bottoms close at hand, and I deal with additional cleaning myself, with "to be thrown in the rubbish bin" option, for safety.

To put his clothes on by himself

Here, too, use a little physical guidance at first, then verbal guidance, and eventually try to let him do alone. At the beginning, lay out his clothes on the floor, on the right side, or teach him to use foolproof devices to find out the right side.

To wash his hands

Break the hand washing actions down: turn on the tap, wet hands, turn off the tap, get soap, rub the backs and the palms of the hands, turn on the tap again, rinse hands, turn off the tap again, get a towel and wipe hands.

You might have to guide your child physically and verbally at first, or provide him a pictogram sequence as a visual guidance. Once he has understood the right order of the actions, reduce guidance.

What's next?

Toilet training and schooling

Toilet training at school is still a concern among parents and teachers. It is very important to deal with this in a book about autonomy and toilet training, because toilet training is acquired only when the child is able to generalize his behaviours everywhere outside his home, including at school.

Your child's rights

In France, despite what some teachers would like us to believe, schools cannot deny access to a child, even if he is not toilet trained. You can insist that he go to school, whether he is toilet trained, partly toilet trained, or not toilet trained at all.

However, I believe such issues have to be settled with wisdom: a schoolteacher, even with a classroom assistant, already has about thirty pupils to deal with; she cannot devote sufficient time to a single pupil, even a disabled one, on each school day.

Whether you decide to send your child to school in his diapers or in his underwear, he will have to be helped by a special needs assistant to keep his dignity. This person will not only help him learn and achieve his exercises; she will help him stay clean and dry, and she will take him to the toilet, as many times as necessary.

The role of the special needs assistant

A special needs assistant is not a babysitter. She is there to help your child acquire a number of skills required by the school; in kindergarten, they primarily focus on skills related to "being a student," which include toilet training.

Your child's special needs assistant could take your child to the toilet regularly. Make her aware of his issues and progress at home, so that she knows what to expect, what she can try, and what she can require from your child.

There is no restricted number of times that the special needs assistant can take your child to the toilet. She has to do it as many times as necessary, to allow your child to be dry and clean, to help him put his clothes on or wipe himself. If you update her on the job you are doing at home and ask her to move in the same direction, she will be able to work on it at the same time as you. It will reinforce your child's acquired skills.

The benefits of imitation

In kindergarten, the opportunity to see that all children of similar age go to the bathroom can be beneficial for an autistic child. Imitation may not be systematic, but it may develop. Being exposed to an environment in which going to the bathroom is something natural that everyone does might release blockages in toilet training acquisition.

Dealing with regression

Regression occurs when your child forgets everything he has learned, either for a rather short period of time, or, as it might unfortunately happen, forever.

Matthieu might have small regressions from time to time in toilet training. It usually occurs when he suffers from toothaches, which cause him diarrhea; he often soils his underpants in those situations.

Dealing with regressions is very difficult. You often feel like your child has lost everything, forever, and suddenly you worry about your future life, having to deal with 40-year-old, 265 lb, 6.2 ft adult you will have to wipe ten times a day.

You should be aware that after a regression, a progress often occurs, because a child cannot do everything at the same time. If you identify the reasons why this regression took place, you will be likely to successfully anticipate the hard times and help your child, so that they last the shortest amount of time possible.

At home, a dose of paracetamol makes toilet training regressions last for much less time than when I forget that he probably soils himself because he suffers from toothaches!

Stop diapers all at once or gradually?

The ideal would be to stop diapers all at once, day and night, but it is not always that easy for parents of autistic children, who already feel exhausted at the end of the day and often have nights of little sleep because their children don't sleep much.

Furthermore, it may be difficult for people who are taking long road trips to ask their child to hold himself, because he might not understand why.

I personally think against the current on that issue: I don't think you really have to stop diapers at once, provided that the child stays in diapers for limited times only (i.e. at night, or during long car trips).

However, every time there is easy access to toilet, you must avoid putting him in diapers, even when you are exhausted, even when you cannot stand it anymore. Gather your courage and continue your efforts! They will pay off eventually, probably sooner than expected!

Should boys pee standing up?

Personally, I don't think it is absolutely necessary to teach little boys to pee standing up, unless you devote most of your time hiking into the wild without a toilet in sight. Boys can pee sitting down on the toilet; it is certainly more convenient for them and for the person who will come and clean up afterwards.

For those who really want it, here are a few tips to help teaching and pointing out:

- Put a little piece of toilet paper in the toilet and ask him to aim at it;

- Add dye into the toilet so that your child can enjoy watching the water change colour;

- Here too, imitation can be useful: show him how Daddy or his classmates do it;

- Let him pee outside, standing behind a line, and see who is peeing the farthest (ask Dad or a classmate for help).

I do believe this is a "non-issue." Either your little boy will learn by himself, on his own or by imitating others, or he never will, which, in my opinion, will not taint his masculinity.

Encourage autonomy

Try to provide less and less assistance to your child on toilet training. You have to be able to trust him gradually; you must know, of course, that he can go to the toilet whenever he wants to, but also that he will be able to manage on his own.

No more diapers; it's time to wear underwear

Matthieu had difficulties in giving up diapers; he tried many times to cheat and put a diaper on after a visit to the bathroom.

In those situations, the only way is to stay firm, to take away his diapers and hide them. Don't give in!

My web articles about toilet training

You will find in the following pages the articles about toilet training I published on my autism website. They are not necessarily dealing with toilet training only, but they indicate my son Matthieu's progress.

Matthieu and Julien are now fully potty trained.

Reduce rituals as much as possible

Rituals and stereotypies are prominent among people with autism. You can try to explain to an adult with autism that he'd better not follow rituals too closely, but it is much more difficult, yet no less important, to do it with a child with autism.

For a long time, Matthieu used to flap his hands every time he was happy; that is, every two minutes (we have a very happy child, which is a good thing, but something had to be done). We requested him many times not to do so and held his hands to stop him, so he eventually almost gave up this ritual. He will still do it once in a while, but it is rare and a simple reminder is enough to make him understand he has to be careful and not do it again.

It took a while, too, but he has almost stopped opening and closing doors and cupboards over and over again, and switching lights on and off repeatedly. At least he no longer does that at home, where I keep a close eye on him all the time. At the childcare center, the childminders are not as strict as I am, so he might do it again several times, even when they prevent him from doing it. Even though they are allowed to be firm and to scold him, even to restrict if necessary, I have noticed he can spend many minutes doing that each time he goes there. Therefore, until they decide to be more firm, he won't stop his stereotypies.

These days, Matthieu requires going to to the bathroom to pee every time we go to a new place. At first, I rejoiced to see he was able to ask to go to the toilet outside the house, but I soon realized it was becoming a ritual. Therefore, I discussed it last week with the therapeutic team, and we decided not to give in when he asked, particularly when he had gone to the toilet before leaving home. The purpose was not to reduce his autonomy in the future, but to make him understand that toilet visits are not compulsory when we go to a new place.

Kindergarten, autism and toilet training

"My son has autism and he is not toilet trained. Can he enter kindergarten anyway?"

Many mothers of very young autistic children ask themselves the same question, and several points must be examined before we can answer it.

First of all, in France, if your child has autism, you have to provide to the school a request for a Special Needs Assistant.

Most classes are provided with a schoolteacher and sometimes a classroom assistant for thirty pupils or so. Therefore they cannot easily deal with an autistic child, because he requires special attention to be able to learn, keep quiet, and stay clean.

The schoolteacher or the classroom assistant cannot leave the classroom and leave all the other pupils alone, especially with that age group, to change the autistic child's diaper; I think it is clear to everyone. He needs someone who will stay by his side during the whole school time. This person is the special needs assistant.

So the answer is yes: your autistic child can enter kindergarten, even if he is not toilet trained, on the express condition that he has been provided with a special needs assistant who will take care of him only, ensure that he is behaving properly and learning like his classmates, and that he is keeping his dignity and is not keeping a dirty diaper all day.

When rituals become troublesome

Matthieu has had a new fad: he goes to the toilet every time he gets outside the house, particularly when go to speech therapy and his psycho-motor therapy sessions. He asks to go to the bathroom as soon as we arrive, and I know for sure that he also asks for a bathroom visit when he is alone with his therapists.

At first, I thought it was a good sign that he was improving in toilet training, but now it is becoming more and more like a ritual. Even though I am happy to see that he can express his needs with words, I tend to refuse bathroom access sometimes, so that it will not become compulsory each and every time we leave home.

Recently, I've cheated, and I've taken him to the toilet before we leave to go to the appointments, so that I can refuse when he asks for toilet visits without feeling too guilty. I keep on allowing him from time to time, so that he won't conclude that he can't go to the bathroom outside the house anymore.

Some tips to help toilet training settle in

I cannot claim I am an expert in toilet training: neither of my two children is toilet trained yet, and I did not assist in anybody's toilet training (I just advised my niece to move her child from potty to toilet).

Yet, I have collected many ideas and pieces of advice on the web, and I decided to summarize them for those among you who will experience this situation after I do.

When is a child ready to be toilet trained?

It is said that the right toilet training age is when the child can walk up and down steps all by himself without stopping at each step. It appears to be a good indication that the sphincter muscles are mature enough to enable the child to hold back.

It is said that a child can be toilet trained just after birth. My personal view on this is that it is the parents who are keeping the baby dry and clean; the baby is not truly toilet trained. In my opinion, a child is toilet trained when he is able to express his urge to go to the potty, or to sit on it by himself. When mom or dad have to remember to sit him regularly for a year or two, I don't call this toilet training, I call this slavery!

It is hard to say when a child is ready to be toilet trained. I think each child reaches this stage in his evolution in his own time, according to his motives. He has to understand how useful potty and toilet are, and he must be willing to comply. Some children who are physically mature may not yet be mentally mature enough. So you have to try regularly, until the day you feel he is ready.

Practical advice for moms

Here are a few ideas to make this task easier for you:

- Restrict your child's mobility and attract him to places that are easy to clean (so that you won't have to clean soiled sheets or a sofa);

- Bring anything that can remove the dirt quickly: toilet paper, cleansing wipes, cotton squares, gloves, cleaning products for babies' bottoms, waterproof undersheet, plastic bags, etc.

- Leave your child bare-bottomed at the beginning: if your child is like mine, at first he will confuse diapers and underpants, and you will probably have to change his underwear quite often. And if he needs to go to the potty and you have to take all his clothes off, he may not be able to hold himself long enough.

- Try to start with a toilet seat insert, so that you will have less to clean up, sometimes children accept it from the start. Yet if he forgets to go, leave the potty in clear view. Moreover, most autistic children are not necessarily able to relate the potty and the toilet, so you may have to start all over again if he wants to use the potty only.

Don't hesitate to do anything that might help to make your task easier! It is not fun to clean your children's excrement off the carpet; let's not make our lives even more complicated, shall we? Choose a time that is convenient for you, and hold on!

Let's put it into perspective!

It is not such a big deal if your child is the last kid in the neighbourhood to achieve toilet training! If your child has autism, there is even more reason to be serene. You must take the time to help your child understand the appropriate use of toilet, and achieve autonomy to go... Stop the stress!

Some tips to help toilet training settle in

I am providing the following pieces of advice just the way they were written when I read them. I don't necessarily follow them (see the reports), but they work for other people, so if you want to try them, go ahead!

- Leave the door open when you go to the toilet. My husband and I are not huge fans of this method, but it can be viable for less uptight parents.

- Learning toilet training in a group. That is what I do with my sons; watching his younger brother using the potty successfully encourages Matthieu to do his best. Competition between siblings can be useful sometimes.

- Avoid any food that causes constipation. It is always easier to get children to go to the bathroom when they don't suffer from bowel problems.

- Suggest some games when he is on the potty. A child who is getting bored won't stay on the potty. I spent many hours staying next to Matthieu, playing games with him (he even learned to say his first words on the toilet!). Julien is easy to please: watching a video on television keeps him quiet for as long as necessary.

- Set up a routine. First, removing one's clothes, then pee/poo-making, then wiping oneself, then putting back one's underpants, toilet-flushing, sticker sticking, getting a sweet. If necessary, help him with such visual cues as pictograms representing the series of actions to be done; you would stick them in the bathroom and review the series with him every time until it becomes an automatic reflex.

- Use food reinforcers. When your child relieves himself in the potty, offer him something to drink or to eat, which not only serves as a good reward, but it allows the machine to work and increase the number of bathroom trips. Practice makes perfect.

- Requesting that he goes to the potty within twenty minutes after a meal. It seems to be the time when the urge to poop arises. I tried it with Julien, who indeed tends to relieve himself every time I get him to nap.

- When an accident occurs, ask your child to help you clean up. It will give him a sense of responsibility, and next time he will try to avoid soiling himself so that he won't have to clean up the mess, which "costs" him.

- Set up a reward system. You won't need to spend a fortune on it: just a few coloured stickers to stick or a stamp pad to use every time your child goes to the toilet successfully will be enough.

- Every time he goes to the toilet, remember to congratulate him warmly. Don't hesitate to make a big fuss about it and tell everybody. Children are attentive when we talk about them, and they are proud when they are told they have done the right thing. Call grandpa and grandma on the phone every day to tell them about your child's progress.

- Set the timer regularly throughout the day. At first it used to ring every ten minutes. Now it rings less frequently (every half an hour or so). It reminds me to suggest that they go to the toilet regularly when I am absorbed in another task.

Some autonomy in toilet training

In the last few days, Matthieu has demonstrated that he can improve and achieve a bit more autonomy in toilet training. It is far from being a spectacular leap, but he has made two little steps up that give me reason to hope for a brighter future.

First, he has achieved more and more autonomy when he uses the toilet: he can remove his trousers and his diaper, sit on the toilet all by himself, urinate, take some sheets of toilet paper and wipe himself, flush the toilet, and put his clothes back on. Usually, I check that he has put his diaper back on correctly.

He has managed to do the whole process by himself twice, which got him warm congratulations. But Matthieu likes me to be with him when he goes to the bathroom. One day, as I sent him to the bathroom all alone, he came back, with his trousers round his ankles, to ask me, "Are you coming?"—which is a huge language leap for a non-verbal child!

For three days now, he has been willing to try to push when he is on the toilet, which he had categorically refused to do since he first tried toilet training. Every time he had to poop he would hide from us, and he was able to hold himself forever when we tried to catch him at the right time and take him to the toilet.

He made a tiny little poop three times, the smallest poop ever, in the toilet. It was too small to fall into the toilet bowl, but it was a giant step anyway. Of course, he was much congratulated for this, was given sweets, and we applauded and we did the dance of victory. Now, we are working hard to have, every evening, a small piece of cleanliness in the toilet, hoping it will become a habit quite soon!

Toilet trained!

After a five-year struggle to teach Matthieu to poop in the toilet, after many refusals and poop smeared on the walls, after roughly 7,500 used diapers... That's it—Matthieu has almost achieved toilet training!

For almost a week, there has been no poop in his diapers, and peeing seems to be under control, too.

We are wondering about the reasons underlying this progress. Matthieu was definitely able to hold back and relieve himself in the toilet, yet he refused to do it. Was there anything in particular that induced him? Or was it a combination of facts that we will never be able to piece together? Eventually, it is not that important.

Today, Matthieu has moved from diapers to underpants. This should put an end to untimely peeing, since now we will see it right away, and we will be able to make him understand that he must not relieve himself in his underwear.

This progress is both wonderful and unexpected. Sometimes, I still wake up at night and tell myself I am dreaming, and yet... I still need some more time to realize that he is actually toilet trained (probably in two weeks, when we will know for sure that he has not soiled himself again). You have the right to pinch me!

I must take this opportunity to give a message of hope for all parents who are still waiting for their children to be toilet trained. I send you many positive vibes and much encouragement: don't give in, repeat your instructions over and over again, insist... It will happen someday!

The underwear wars

Four days ago, it had been two weeks since Matthieu had pooped in his diaper. I therefore decided to put him in underpants, so that we could work on full daytime toilet training (I still leave him in diapers at night).

Matthieu can tell me when he wants to go to the toilet, and for the moment, I am letting him go when he has decided to, without any particular schedule. I just tell him to remember to go when he has not gone to the toilet for a long time, or when I see him so absorbed in a game that he may "forget" that he no longer wears diapers.

But this morning, Matthieu has decided that he does not want to wear underpants anymore. Maybe it is because the last time he had an accident, I told him we were going to spend a few days without video games, because when he plays these games he tends to forget to go to the toilet.

Or maybe he considers diapers something that enable him to relieve himself wherever he wants to? I don't know, but I won't give in on this issue anyway, and I will hold out against his willingness to give up wearing underpants.

First round: Matthieu refuses to put his underpants on. Of course, I don't intend to yield to Matthieu's rigidity; I encourage him and insist that he wear his underpants. Matthieu grumbles, but complies.

Second round: Matthieu hides his underpants in the middle of the piles of diapers, and puts a diaper on, under his trousers, in hopes that I won't realize and put a diaper on him without thinking! So I go and fish out the underpants from where he hid them and puts them back on him while he shouts at me.

Third round: I find Matthieu sitting on the bathroom floor, struggling to put a diaper on all by himself. What a stubborn child! It was very cute, and I laughed so hard.

Still, I am very proud of my son; he proved he was capable of such tours de force as becoming toilet trained suddenly, on a whim, while we had almost ceased to believe it was possible. Consenting to wear underwear is just a small step, a tiny mile in the marathon he has run already. I am sure that by the opening day of school, we won't hear anymore about daytime pee accidents. Congratulations to you, Matthieu!

Being toilet trained outside the home, too: generalization

The issue with autistic children is that they can achieve something successfully in a specific place, such as being toilet trained at home, but once they are in a different place or a different context, lose this skill.

After eventually having understood the process of using the toilet, having struggled to introduce a little autonomy, Matthieu succeeded in toilet training last week. No more accidents! Above all, when outside the house, at school or when we visit friends, he stays clean and uses the toilet available, which was not exactly a done deal before.

Now we have to try toilet training while on the road (we have long road trips, and one and a half hour's drive seems a bit long to me, so we will start with short trips) and night time toilet training (but we will wait until the weather gets warmer, to avoid dressing and undressing sessions in the middle of the night).

Thanks to everyone who encouraged and supported us during these last months, we eventually made it! I am extremely proud of my son, and I am looking forwards to hearing about your children's successes too.

Toilet training: when it turns into a nightmare

There are times when toilet training may turn into a nightmare! I receive the following question a few days ago:

"My daughter has developed a ritual of relieving herself on her bedroom floor in the evening. What can I do to stop such an annoying ritual?"

I think I will remember the weeks before Matthieu became fully toilet trained for the rest of my life. He had achieved daytime dryness, but he absolutely refused to poop in the toilet. Until then, I was just getting angry every time I saw his diaper full of poop, but I wasn't out of the woods yet!

Then suddenly, Matthieu must have felt filling his diaper wasn't enough, he also had to spread his poop on his fingers, on his face -- on the wall, on his sheets! You can imagine the horror, especially when it happened several times a day!

I don't have a universal answer to help you on this issue. As for me, I tried to make this behaviour as costly as possible. Since cleaning up the floor was fun to him and my neutral expression did not cause any improvement, I got very angry and took him to the toilet for increasingly longer periods of time. Instead of doing an activity that was fun to him, he found himself scolded and punished in a place that was no fun (toys and reinforcers have been moved away, of course).

Then, strangely, after this huge regression, Matthieu became clean, fully toilet trained, during daytime and at night. A huge regression is often followed by huge progress. By the way, when we moved, Matthieu, who had achieved daytime dryness for more than a month, started to wet his underpants again. We had to show him again that it was an unacceptable behaviour so that he would resume, faster this time, the habit of relieving himself in the toilet.

Autism, school, and toilet training: diapers or underwear?

Toilet training, whether at home or at school, is a really difficult issue when related to autism. I really feel that it remains a key concern until it is acquired. Here is a question I received about toilet training at school:

"I've got a four-year-old son who has atypical autism. He has achieved dryness, but he refuses to use the potty or the toilet to poop. The schoolteacher has asked me to put him in diapers when he goes to school. What should I do?"

I know that French schools have no legal right to refuse your child if he is not clean yet, particularly because, since he has a disability and he has not achieved toilet training, he is entitled to the support of a Special Needs Assistant to help him learn and keep his dignity (and avoid spending the whole day in a soiled diaper).

We are always recommended getting rid of diapers completely when we start toilet training our children, so I guess that doing otherwise would "break" toilet training somehow. However, to be friendly with the teaching team, I think it's better to keep your child in diapers when he is at school, and to require that he be taken to the toilet regularly.

As for me, I understood perfectly how useful it could be to comply with such a request when my son Matthieu went to school, last year, even though he wasn't toilet trained yet. First, putting hands in poop is not really pleasant for the people who take care of your child (nor is it for us, let's be honest about it). Secondly, diapers hold a large amount of poop, whereas it goes through underwear. So your child may soil everything around him, which will cause you problems with the school administration or other pupils' parents. In my opinion, avoiding problems is the best thing to do.

Finally, there is a greater risk of taunting or bullying from other children if he relieves himself in his underwear than if he is in diapers. Our children need to socialize with other children; things will go much better if they are not repulsed by the idea of approaching our offspring.

Putting Matthieu in diapers did not prevent him from achieving toilet training later. Something clicked, maybe because he saw the other children poop in the toilet, but we don't really know what actually decided him.

Moreover, children can understand the context: during school time or at night, they are in diapers. During long car trips, they are in diapers. Even though things are more difficult for a child with autism, he will eventually understand the context at some point, and probably the reason why he has to wear a diaper too. This is another important step towards achieving toilet training: understanding what has to be done, what must not be done, what other people do, etc.

But as soon as your child agrees to poop in the potty or in the toilet more or less regularly (for example, he still has some accidents, but he has relieved himself in the right place for two weeks), insist that he no longer wears diapers at school. Children who may have accidents and children who would inevitably soil themselves should not be treated in the same way.

Toilet training: struggling against refusals and giving the keys to autonomy

Well, we are certainly talking a lot about toilet training these days! I received recently this letter about toilet training, refusals and lack of autonomy:

"My five-year old son has not worn diapers in the daytime for five and a half years. And yet, he almost never goes to the toilet alone: we have to take him to the toilet, and quite often, to force him to go. Is there a way to help him?"

I have been rather lucky with Matthieu's autonomy and refusals. Matthieu is a little boy who has a thirst for autonomy, and it is easy to entrust him with such tasks as asking to go to the toilet when he feels the urge to (I am currently focusing on teaching him to go without requesting my permission when at home).

What if an autistic child refuses to go to the toilet?

My first reaction is to hold firm. Toilet visits should not be suggested as a choice, but as a requirement, to avoid tantrums. However, if your child is sensitive to this, you can temporize:

- By telling him there will be compulsory toilet visits before or after each meal, for example, or any other significant daily event, so that it eventually becomes a (good) habit.

- To focus on physical signs of discomfort (feet stamping, pulling his underwear) to teach your child to identify the times when he must go to the toilet.

- Let him know a few minutes before: "You can play your game for another five minutes, then you'll go to the toilet." Use a timer if necessary. Autistic children do not like unpredictability that much, so it is better to leave some sort of "buffer" between the time of the request and the time to do it.

Then you can set up a system of rewards. For example, for each toilet visit completed without any fuss, he will be allowed a sweet or any mini-reinforcer he would enjoy. Then to get others, he will have to go five times in succession without any refusal, then ten times, and so on, until you can deal with another issue. For example, each time he peed in the toilet successfully, Matthieu was allowed to stick a coloured sticker on a paper on the toilet wall. Gradually, we began to use it for poop only, and now we do not use it at all.

How can autonomy be fostered in toilet visits?

The first question that comes to mind is: does your child feel the urge to go to the toilet, and does he look embarrassed when he is wet or soiled? A child who does not care if his bottom is in pee and poop might not see the need to go to the toilet. My answer to this question is based on the assumption that your child enjoys being dry and clean.

Then, as with refusals, you have to foster autonomy by starting with an habit that your child might assimilate later to gain a little more spontaneity. First, point out to him the physical signs of discomfort when he is wiggling or pulling his trousers and suggest that he go to the toilet. Stay near him, but don't help him.

Whether your child can pull on/take off his clothes all by himself or not, your presence should become increasingly less necessary. Some children will learn to manage on their own quickly, whereas it will take much longer for others. What matters is that no regression occurs, always improvements; stagnation stages are normal in a child's development.

Each action has to be broken down into steps: open the bathroom door, enter the bathroom, turn on the light, pull down one's pants, pull down one's underpants, sit down on the toilet, relieve oneself, wipe oneself, pull one's underwear back on, then one's pants, flush the toilet, wash one's hands, turn off the light, leave the bathroom, close the door, etc.

When your child needs help, use physical guidance, then gradually, when he can achieve one step of the action by himself, just guide him verbally and remind him the next stages. Don't hesitate to tell him the next action several times in succession if he does not understand the first time; if necessary, when you notice that verbal instruction has not been fully understood or connected with the gesture that has to be achieved, initiate a light physical guidance if it can help him understand (i.e.: tucking his finger into the waistband of his pants and make repeated pushes downward, while repeating verbal instruction).

I would like to emphasise the necessity of always giving the same verbal instruction, over time and regardless who is taking care of the child. This is an important point that facilitates understanding. If the child understands the instruction when given by one person but not by another, then work as a pair for some time until the child assimilates the different voices and understands that in both cases, the order is the same.

Once the first gestures are fully understood, take an increasingly longer time to take your child to the bathroom. For example, if he has learned the series "open the door/turn on the toilet light/pull down his trousers," don't go with him, but try to foresee the moment when he will need your help and come help him at that time only. If he has to wait a little bit, it is not a big deal; it might give him the incentive to carry on the process all by himself. Otherwise, show your surprise if he has not completed the next stage yet ("Why haven't you pulled down your underpants yet?") and remind him the next verbal instruction ("Come on, pull down your underpants!").

Now Matthieu just has to learn not to ask for permission each and every time he wants to go to the toilet. He can feel when it is the right time to go, he is able to go all by himself, relieve himself, wipe himself all alone and, most of the time, he can pull his clothes back on too (sometimes he asks me to help him get his trousers on so they aren't on backwards).

During this learning period, don't hesitate to give your clothes that are easy to put on and put off to your child. No need to complicate the task; later he will have the opportunity to understand how zippers and snaps work.

The unexplainable link between teething and toilet training

I must admit it, I still cannot explain it, and as soon as tomorrow I'm going to talk about it to Matthieu's therapists, but there seems to be a direct link between eruption of permanent teeth and toilet training.

Sensitive souls, brace yourselves: it's going to be about excrement... Sorry!

Some time ago, Matthieu has cut his first permanent tooth. By the way, I am surprised I did not write an article on this (I am going senile). We could see clearly the concern on his face, until we told him not to worry, that it happened because he is growing up (Matthieu likes to be told he is a big boy because it means more privileges for him), that all children lose their teeth, that they fall out because bigger ones are growing underneath.

To cut a long story short, the first milk tooth was recovered successfully, the tooth fairy came, joy, happiness, and fireworks. Then suddenly, at the same time, there were what I would call "skid marks" on Matthieu's briefs. It did not last long, so everything quickly returned to normal, and I stopped thinking about it.

A few days ago, the skid marks came back more obviously. And it seems that a new permanent tooth is growing under the others. I can tell you this because I've checked, and when I tried to recall the last time Matthieu soiled his briefs, I remembered it was when he cut his first permanent tooth. Matthieu had been clean from one day to another, and had very few accidents.

Once, twice... We came to a situation in which we had to change his underpants every 15 minutes! We found ourselves sliding into a spiral of horror, imagining ourselves putting him back in diapers (I had to put a diaper on him at night after he soiled almost all his briefs and trousers, and his bed linen too).

We asked ourselves many questions:

- Has anything changed since he was toilet trained (the answer is yes, he got an MP3 player for Christmas and listens to it in his bedroom; he could have been too absorbed and forgot to go to the toilet. But even after the MP3 player was taken away, the behaviour continued).
- Is there a problem with his diet?
- Does he want to be like his brother, who is still relieving himself in his diaper?
- Is he ill? Does he suffer anywhere?

We even thought about the possibility that he might have associated the onset of toothaches with the fact of growing up, and that he had decided to relieve himself in his underpants to "stay small" and prevent his permanent teeth from growing.

I firmly believe his permanent teeth are causing him pain, which is the reason for this current carelessness. In fact, when I give him paracetamol, we have fewer skid marks, which gives credence to my theory. I will probably have more clarification tomorrow.

YOUR IDEAS, MEMORIES AND TRICKS

This section is yours. Write down your ideas, your child's progress about toilet training.

ABOUT THE AUTHOR

Nathalie Aynié

I write about autism from the heart: my two sons have a form of autism, and I am—self-diagnosed —on the spectrum too.

I strive to provide tips for parents to help their children to become autonomous as soon as possible.

Please register to my mailing-list to be informed when another book will be available:

http://nathalieaynie.com/autism-mailing-list

Made in United States
Orlando, FL
29 July 2023

35570667R00067